AF373888

Table of contents

2 secret of your success

Confidence

Your second secret to success is Confidence

- It is necessary to overcome laziness, indecision, own weaknesses.

- Overcome the evil influences of those around you

- It is important to develop life experience, skills and abilities, this is the basis of confidence, future success and prosperity.

The real confidence that is necessary in life comes as a result of overcoming one's own weaknesses, working on oneself, and does not depend on the opinions of others. Such a person will be respected in any robot and in any company.

Developing good qualities is the same as putting money into a bank account at high interest rates.

We continue to understand what self-esteem and self-confidence really are. You need to know and understand this so that you achieve good self-esteem and strong self-confidence. In other words, in order to master the path, you need to know where to go.

Confidence development

Have you done something recently that gives you confidence? Something simple that gave you a feeling of satisfaction, self-confidence, or maybe even led to gratitude from a friend or family member? Of course, you have such moments - so, remember this feeling and try to put yourself in situations that will again give you this good feeling. We all need to build trust by fulfilling tasks, both simple and complex, which leads to greater confidence and, in turn, to great achievements.

Everyone, whether qualified or professional, at some point lacks self-confidence. And we all need to overcome the frustration, indecision, laziness and bad influence of some of the so-called "friends" and peers that lead us from this critical quality called confidence. Sir Edmund Hillary, a famous climber, said that this is best: "We are not defeating Everest, but ourselves." Fortunately for us, we don't need to go out and climb the highest mountain in the world every day.

"You must not be great to begin, but you must begin to be great."

Zig Ziglar

What we all need to do to succeed in this magical time is the development of life experience and positive qualities (look at this as "lending" money to your savings account at high interest rates), which give us a wider basis of trust . This experience can be fun and will certainly lead to personal development and greater confidence at the same time. Let's make a simple list to get started:

These qualities will make you confident and lead the development up:

(1.) Read more books, namely in the direction of training, knowledge and motivation
(2.) Develop your creativity in an art class
(3.) Do physical exercises, go to yoga, dance to the gym or swim (if you are not in shape, start with a few steps, and soon you will see a positive result and your confidence with this will also increase)
(4.) Communicate with wise, experienced people and trainers (their depth of experience and knowledge of proven methods will certainly be useful to you)
(5.) Do good deeds (helping others who are less fortunate than you, or who just need help, will surely bring you a sense of confidence and satisfaction).
(6.) Lovely
(7.) Goal setting
(8.) Fulfillment of promises
(9.) Cleanliness

"All dignity, all strength is calm - precisely because they are confident in themselves."

-Vissarion Belinsky

How long does it take to succeed?

Although this sometimes happens, it seems "instant" or "waving a magic wand" for almost everything. Those who were successful were ready for success, and it was then that they thought about their own development, and they prepared to become students in the form of personal development.

Well, it's time to leave the popcorn, stop playing with the computer and turn off the phone in order to access the five specific components in order to be successful. It has been said many times, and here it will be repeated again.

Success is a choice, and you can choose to be successful, or you can decide to fail again, the good news is that the choice is yours. And you can choose the right path every day and this is good news for you.

Personal development is really a general description of the many small changes and decisions that are made every day in your life for your personal success. There is a law to attract success in your life, and I will tell you about it below.

Now you can achieve success by following the simple recommendations below, the main thing is to do them regularly. If you really want to succeed. make sure that you follow these instructions and apply them for yourself and your success:

1. Daily meditation / visualization of goals

Specific purpose and daily review; visualize your specific, measurable, achievable, relevant and timely goals with the feeling that you have already achieved them. A simple but very effective technique will help you in visualization.

Make a visualization board and place all your goals on it. It is also imperative to celebrate those goals that you have already achieved, to increase self-confidence. I described in detail how to achieve my goals in the book "A COMPLETE GUIDE FOR DETERMINING AND SETTING THE GOALS OF LIFE".

2. Daily activities that generate income

Can you do something? Something that will now generate revenue correctly? If you think that you can relax and let it go, or if you do not devote enough work to thinking that you have not yet reached the ideal to do this work, you are wasting your time. As Mike Litman says: "You don't have to do it right, you just have to start doing it!"

3. Engage in personal development

You can begin to connect yourself with the study of personal development, if you do not, you just become a reflection of what you are connected with (media, computer games, the negative influence of friends and everything else that depresses you, puts you back and makes you stay in a swamp). They are the one product that allows you to be destroyed in the mind.

4. Learn from the masters and leaders

Successful people have mentors and trainers in the field where they want to succeed, people who want to learn and share knowledge and positively charge. As soon as you receive them, do not let go! If you let them escape, they will not wait until you catch up with them and ask them to teach. You need to take the initiative yourself, and asks for students.

5. Maintain the expectation of leadership

Leaders go in front and do not look back and do not stop at their mistakes. First, strive for excellence in your industry and do what you need to do every day. Therefore, you can expect the same from others; people who succeed and contribute to success through your influence and example. These people will follow you because you want guidance and success in you and those around you.

6. Consider every day as a very vital day, and be prepared to push every day

Go boldly every day, knowing that you should not strain very much but you must fully use all available minutes, opportunities and resources to achieve the desired result. Every time you start to relax or switch to autopilot mode, you immediately begin to lose a valuable impulse and know that it may be more difficult to return this impulse than you think. Commit and then keep yourself accountable - your success depends on it.

7. Champions work more

The philosophy is simple and means finding more ways to do more - either in the gym, on the pitch, or in a team. Champions work more than others. When people start something new, bright and promising, at first they are driven by enthusiasm, mixed in with emotions. After a while, the euphoria disappears. Routine and boredom appear. And with them a drop in interest in the case. The emphasis on much-needed improvements at any given time, and the creation of a continuous learning environment underlies the most successful people culture. "When it's hard for me, I always remind myself that if I give up, it won't get any better," said world boxing legend Mike Tyson. "The most difficult fight is when you have to fight laziness for happiness," said another legend, Mohammed Ali.

Summary:

Although there is no guarantee in life; You can follow the above components to succeed and apply them consistently in your life. If you do, you will get everything you want! Success and the time needed for success ... Now you have to understand; The result is completely up to you!

Is there 100% self-confidence and 100% strong self-esteem?

First of all, you need to understand that doubt is normal and natural. But the complete categoricality and lack of doubt is not entirely normal and in no way is a high self-esteem and self-confidence.

If you notice that there are narrowly specialized experts, they have powerful self-confidence and self-esteem in any expert subject determined by them. But - they listen to you, accept your arguments, and are ready to object to them constructively, logically, challenge, dispute, etc. This is not blind self-confidence.

We live in a reality in which there is nothing at 100%, there is no 100% guarantee in anything, except for one - the only 100% guaranteed event - we will all die sooner or later. And you should not demand 100% certainty from yourself and you have to be very careful with those who are 100% confident in something - this is either fanaticism or DECEPTION.

If you have doubts, you are not sure about something - this does not mean that you have low self-esteem or that you are doing something wrong. But now, if someone assures you of something 100%, this most likely means that you are being deceived. Many people want to be deceived - this removes responsibility, relaxes, the truth shortens life.

Typically, politicians, officials, lawyers, and many employers show 100% confidence - which is a sign that they are cheating - you probably often managed to make sure of this.

Confucius, said that only at age 60 he learned to distinguish when he was deceived. It is not easy to learn, it takes years - do not demand perfectionism from yourself

15 secrets to increasing self-esteem and self-confidence - a step-by-step plan.

Applying at least some of the tips and even slightly increasing self-confidence and self-esteem, you will greatly simplify your life, increase your income, improve the well-being and quality of your life in general! You can achieve this quickly and easily.

Why is it important? Or what is self-confidence?

Your life success = Your Professionalism / skills, multiplied by Self-confidence and self-esteem. Which means that you cannot compensate for new knowledge and professionalism - a lack of confidence and self-esteem. If you want to live better and earn more - develop your self-confidence and self-esteem.

Have you noticed that there are not very smart, but successful people who are self-confident, perhaps impudent, rude, stick forward like a bulldozer and strangely enough, for some reason, achieve what they want?

And vice versa, there are very smart, kind people, perhaps with 2-3 higher educations, but unsuccessful, because they are unsure of themselves and with low self-esteem? And so that they do not - somehow it doesn't work out very well, falls out of hand. It is not a matter of professional knowledge, besides they still need courage, pressure, determination.

That's what the presence or absence of self-confidence and good self-esteem means. You cannot compensate them - having received the next university or MBA diploma by reading the next hundred books.

I know excellent, kind, beautiful people, with three higher educations living in cities who can hardly earn money for their own food, because they have great self-doubt and low self-esteem.

Having even a small grain of self-confidence - you can "move mountains" of affairs. And it's really easy to realize, develop in yourself.

Tip 1: Uncertainty and low self-esteem - no need to be ashamed.

We live in a very difficult time and go through several structural crises at once. We were not prepared at school for such difficult times and quick changes. Therefore, economic crises are called depressions.

They hit painfully in self-esteem and self-confidence of almost all people. Not even businessmen can stand it. Stress, chronic fatigue and burnout are becoming the main diseases that lead to heart disease, cancer, and even death.

Shame - crowds out a problem from consciousness. In other words, what are you ashamed of - you try not to notice, not talk about it and not pay attention to it. The problem will remain, only you will not notice it and will not know what you are suffering from. For example, I spent three years to understand what was happening - I was ashamed. During this time, one could become self-confident dozens of times and increase self-esteem. And forget about it.

Life with low self-esteem - creates a risk to health and life in modern conditions. Therefore, it is vital to understand how to increase self-esteem and self-confidence. Fear, shame and laziness - the eyes are large. Everything is much simpler than it seems that the path will be overpowered by the going, and luck is a reward for courage.

Tip 2: Perfectionism or learn to live with self-doubt and low self-esteem.

Even many celebrities admit that they consider themselves not very confident people. Which does not prevent them from succeeding. There is no limit to perfection. There is no limit to self-confidence. The theme is natural for everyone - just everyone has their own level.

One lacks the confidence and self-esteem to find a normal job. For others, to take the business to a new level, earn another million, implement a grandiose project.

Uncertainty and low self-esteem will always bother a little - this is normal. We are all living people. Once you reach your current goal, you will want more and again will not have enough self-esteem and self-confidence for a new goal.

Learn not to worry about uncertainty and learn to keep moving forward in a low self-esteem state! There are no ideal conditions, and they are not needed. Pass the next step and do not even notice how confidence, and self-esteem pulled themselves up.

Tip 3: Why don't most trainings work? Psychology of self-confidence and self-esteem.

Uncertainty and low self-esteem - this is a very deep subconscious habit, which you developed and, alas, took root for decades. And then, through negative experience and stress, they were literally "concreted" in the subconscious. We are controlled by the subconscious and habits - you need to change them first of all.

Work on changes must be carried out at two levels - at the conscious and subconscious levels. At a conscious level, for example, using self-hypnosis, a quick effect is obtained, but short and you have to constantly do self-hypnosis exercises or others. Only at a subconscious level can you produce profound changes and consolidate the result forever.

Most of the trainings that I saw do not work on how to increase self-esteem and self-confidence on a subconscious level. Trainers simply do not know how to work with the subconscious. Well, or they are too lazy to bother. And practice, one way or another, is more like self-suggestion - self-esteem "bursts" like a soap bubble from the very first difficulty.

It's much easier, in one day to create a short-term surge of confidence - quickly get great video reviews. The student will leave satisfied, but after 2 days, confidence and self-esteem fall below the plinth. This does not bother the trainer anymore - the review has been received and will be used to sell the course to other such people.

Attempts to contact the trainer again may result in a hint "that he is a fool", "do further exercises", pay again. This may be repeated several times. The student, having wasted money, remains stupid and continues to soar over the same situations, but with ineffective exercises.

Tip 4: What should be the training? Secrets of the psychology of confidence and self-esteem.

A training that truly teaches how to increase self-esteem and self-confidence and leads to long-term and profound changes:

1. It lasts from 1 month to form the habit of thinking in a new way, the skills to stop doubting and fearing.

2. Contains exercises of meditation for the formation of changes and reinforcing the skill "stop being afraid", doubt the level of consciousness and subconsciousness.

3. Has exercises that let go of previous negative experiences and doubts that concrete self-esteem below the baseboard.

4. Improves life already literally within a month, and even increase the income of the participant.

5. Tips and exercises should be simple. So that even the most insecure get the result, stupidly performing exercises. The number of completed exercises goes into quality - the skills of internal confidence and strong self-esteem are formed.

6. Should not take a lot of time and a lot of effort. They simply do not have a modern person. About 1 hour a day, no more.

7. The "shell" of tension - is released? (The "carapace" of tension - constantly tense muscles on the body on the lower back, shoulders, neck, hips, face - everyone has, but not everyone feels it) If not, then this is not a training on personal growth, but rubbish, with loss time and money. The effect will be short-term - a few days-weeks, a maximum of a month.

8. High-quality formation of new behavioral skills at the subconscious level - through simple exercises.

Exercise 1: You as an asset. How to develop self-confidence and increase self-esteem based on previous experience.

The name suggests a solution. People with low self-esteem and self-doubt do not value themselves, their experience, their knowledge, their past achievements, their skills.

They say - "well, it happened by chance, I was just lucky", "oh yes this is nonsense." They just forget that randomness is not accidental.

If you yourself do not value yourself and your achievements - who else will value you? From the first you learn to value yourself, and then others around you will catch up.

Get a notebook that will be your "success diary." There is something magical in keeping your diary - just keeping a diary you can achieve steady personal growth, develop the skill of analyzing situations, changing yourself, forming the desired qualities of character.

Remember your past experience and life stages: work, youth, university studies, school in different classes.

What were your successes, successes, victories, awards, achievements, skills, positive personal qualities? What obstacles did you overcome to get them? Write it all along with success in your diary.

• What did you do well?

• What did you do, "did your own hands?"

• What could you do for free?

• What activities do you lose your sense of time for?

• What delighted you?

• What caused your eyes to burn in childhood or youth, and your heart began to beat in pleasant excitement?

Write down everything you remember in your notebook. Consciousness is able to displace (forget) minor events. And such events are definitely underestimated. You will need several attempts to remember everything and do not need to demand from yourself to remember everything now. Just do this exercise for several days. As something remembered, write down.

Exercise - Daily Experience.

People tend to pay more attention to negative events and forget, belittle their dignity. It is recommended that every day, mentally walk through the events of the day, remember what you did today. Recall your little daytime victories that you did not notice during the day, good luck, new opportunities, qualities.

Perform the exercise for several weeks or even months until you have a stable skill, a new habit of noticing immediately and appreciating any small achievements of yours, noticing even small opportunities.

You will be surprised how effective it is for you. It is from these "small" achievements that a strong self-confidence is formed, a steady high self-esteem and a successful life are developed.

Exercise 2: Subconscious changes or how to gain self-confidence and increase self-esteem deep inside.

Do you have resentment, doubt? For example, I considered myself not a touchy person. But everything turned out exactly the opposite. I was very touchy and in fact was offended even on the smallest occasion. Gradually, an understanding came that this was not normal and that it was only in me. He began to gradually release insults.

Remember the movie Gentlemen of Fortune? One of the main characters was constantly offended by the other: "I tell him - I have the flu, and he: - Get into the water, get into the water!" Because of this resentment, he forgot that he was forced to climb into the water to hide the same golden helmet. Which they could not remember where they hid and found, the whole film.

So in life, because of grievances, we focus on the bad, and lose sight of the opportunity. And over time, it hits self-esteem.

First, I wrote down in my diary all the insults that bothered me at the moment, and that I could remember. Gained 10-30 grievances. Then he let go of the list. Then he wrote down again and again, and let go until he let go of everything. A strong skill has now formed and I need exactly a couple of seconds to let go of resentment.

How much easier it has become to live and communicate with other people.

The times when I was offended - I remember with horror. Letting go of insult is an indescribable relief. Take a diary, write down 10-30 + insults, start letting them go from the easiest to the most difficult. With every released resentment, you can find a drop of self-confidence and a little increase self-esteem.

- You can only offend the weak.

Is it possible to offend a strong, confident with a strong self-esteem? It turns out that any resentment initially positions you in weakness, vulnerability, and untouchability. To let go of insult means to regain your strength, self-esteem, self-esteem and self-confidence that you can handle it. How nice to be strong from the inside and gain self-confidence and well-deserved self-esteem.

- All insults are such trifles - complete nonsense.

Stop making yourself a sissy - you are much stronger than you seem. Life can ask you a thrash and kicks, so what? Is it worth it to be offended at every occasion? Kick in the ass, means a step forward. The kick is not so terrible as our consciousness paints it. The discomfort from some situations is greatly exaggerated by our consciousness.

And do not waste precious strength on them - offended. Start to let go of grievances, and see how you will become much stronger than yourself. Let go of resentment for yourself, not for someone else. You need it first. Others do not care about your insults - they carry water to those who are offended. Perform the exercise, get rid of grievances, and on your back they will "stop carrying water."

You will gain your strength, become confident with a strong self-esteem.

Exercise 3: Mistakes in life or how to be confident in yourself, increase self-esteem and love yourself, despite past experience.

The world is so arranged that everything is known in comparison. Achievements and victories are therefore valuable because losses can be painful. Again, we are not taught and prepared for a real and harsh life. Yes, it is a beautiful world - but it is full of dangers. Society - the same jungle with the struggle for survival, only tougher. And all life is a struggle: with sleep, with your weaknesses, with challenges, and with anything else ...

If you succeeded, then you received some benefit or reward. If you made a mistake and made a mistake, it means you have learned a life lesson. If you want to achieve success in life - you need to increase the number of mistakes. Without errors, you cannot succeed.

Exercise: Written in writing errors that bother you.

What lesson have you learned from this mistake? Yes, maybe it was painful - take the lesson and release the insult, to the situation, to yourself or others for what happened. This is the stage in life that you need to go through. Take the lesson and move on.

Everyone is wrong. But not everyone is obsessed with mistakes. Rejecting a painful "lesson" - you will attract similar situations over and over again. Having accepted the lesson, you return your strength, self-esteem, self-confidence that you can achieve what you want and go to a new level. Having accepted the situation, you acknowledge that you are stronger than you thought about yourself. The way it is.

Release all your mistakes and move on to new heights. This is exactly how strength is gained, strong life skills, and this is how self-confidence and self-esteem are forged and tempered.

Exercise 4: The roles you play. How to become a confident person and increase self-esteem.

We all play some kind of role. For example, I played a role for a long time, a pretty guy, a kind, funny perky guy. Still - it was so liked by others. Others play roles - I don't care, I don't need anything, I'm the most important, I'm cool / cool. All these roles are not yours and are imposed in the process of socialization. Outwardly, they can be manifested in the choice of clothes, gait, gestures, facial expressions, behavior.

Naturally, the role prevents you from being yourself. By itself - to show their strength. For example, playing the role of a good guy, I could not say "no" - I am a good guy — they used me accordingly. And at a certain point, I decided to change the role of a good guy to a rebel, but this happened when I already reached a certain confidence in myself. Playing in some roles creates the illusion of security, that everything is in order and this is absolutely normal.

In fact, playing a role creates a rejection of a part of yourself, naturally this leads to an underestimation of self-esteem and self-confidence if this is the role of the victim. Rejecting the role of the victim - you regain yourself, gain yourself, your strength, self-confidence. You allow yourself to claim that you really want deep down!

Look into your past. What roles have you played or can you play now? Why do you think you are playing this role? What are you running from hiding in this role? What do you give up on yourself playing this role? What are you afraid of and hiding behind this role? Describe how you should behave in such situations in order to be yourself?

Write it down in a diary, in more detail. Create a mood for yourself that next time you will behave in a new way - as you wrote yourself in a notebook. And you will become more confident in yourself and increase your self-esteem at the deepest subconscious level.

Exercise 5: Unfinished business. Performance. Imitation of violent activity.

Unfinished business draws strength, health and reduces your productivity from you. It's impossible to deceive yourself or your subconscious - the subconscious or some inner part of yourself always knows who you really are.

If you are trying to get some kind of new contract, customer or workplace, but at the same time you have a bunch of unfinished business behind your back, then your subconscious mind will slow you down. As if hinting - well, where are you doing a new job if you have not finished the old? You can't do it. And it will begin to fill you with doubts.

Incomplete situations keep you in the past and prevent you from living. Incomplete relationships - interfere with personal life and are not allowed to create new relationships. Without letting go of unnecessary people - you do not let the right people into your life. This all reduces your self-esteem and self-confidence.

Sometimes it's very difficult to let go of something or someone.

I remember I could not let go of some situation and turned to my teacher with this. Let go of the situation - do not waste your health and strength on it.

Do the exercise as quickly as possible: write down in your diary what unfinished business, relationships, situations you have? Think about how you could finish them to free yourself. Write down your new steps in order to complete the situation. Take action immediately. Release those you need to let go.

You do this for yourself first of all, and not for someone. Create a mood for the future that you will finish situations, projects, work. Stick to this new rule. Remember - you have no restrictions except those. What you yourself have created. You are the very person who most of all holds you back.

Exercise 6: Health effects of uncertainty and low self-esteem.

People with low self-esteem and self-doubt - are inclined to treat themselves, their lives, and their health disdainfully and disregard. Low self-esteem and self-doubt create a state of apathy. They beat off the desire to do something for themselves. Include ignoring yourself.

Some revenge on oneself is even possible. For example, one of my acquaintances at a time of hopelessness could have a drink, and then get behind the wheel and drive around the city "under the hood". Well, this is her form of self-hypnosis, self-punishment for the fact that something does not work out in life. There are other forms that I will not describe.

Remember that health must be monitored. Neglecting one's health is tantamount to neglecting oneself. If you yourself do not value yourself - who will appreciate you? And at the same time, appreciating yourself and your health is almost the same. Be sure to take care of your health - do regular exercises - it's not difficult.

In a healthy body healthy mind. Healthy mind means healthy self-esteem and self-confidence. Take care of your health and do not wait for better times - start taking care of yourself today and every day.

Exercise 7: Stop feeling sorry for yourself

There is such a pattern in behavior - self-pity. Oh, what a pain self-pity brings. Self-pity literally blocks your progress, and kills self-confidence and good self-esteem.

Also self-pity greatly annoys people around. It is incredibly difficult to communicate with such people. Therefore, people subconsciously shun those who feel sorry for themselves; they subconsciously want to get rid of them as quickly as possible. Run away on. Surprisingly - people do not like to be miserable, but often fall into self-pity, they want to be pitied.

Which means that they will look miserable, though logically few can connect this. Get rid of this relic, hard times. If you want to really succeed, then stop feeling sorry for yourself. Success must be taken by strength, firmness, character.

Letting go of self-pity - you regain your strength, restore and strengthen your self-confidence, increase your self-esteem.

Write in a notebook for which you feel sorry for yourself? And start to paint why you really feel sorry for yourself? Release pity until a strong skill is formed. Over time, you can let go of pity in a few seconds. And there will be a habit to stop feeling sorry for yourself.

Exercise 8: Look Into Fear in the Eyes

All people have fears and are afraid of something. We need fear to survive - it is a harbinger of danger. Rational in your fear no more than 1-3 percent.

And everything else that you are afraid of is dust, nothing. The remaining 97% of your fear is an exaggeration. Fear constrains and impedes action. What self-esteem can there be if there are fears? Fear is deposited on the body - a thick layer of tension. Letting go of fear, the tension on the body is also released.

Fear is our first enemy to be defeated. But if you lose to fear, then the loss will be for life. Look deep into fear. Understand - what are you really afraid of. Write it in detail in the diary.

Imagine what happens if something happens that scares you of fear? Is it really as terrible as fear betrays? Do you really not get over it? Keep looking "in the face" of fear and try to understand, feel what you are really afraid of. Write down all your thoughts.

Fear is a harbinger of danger, which without fear we will not notice.

Exercise 9: Release Guilt

As Confucius said: "He who imposes a feeling of guilt on you wants to command you." Feeling guilty literally hammers self-esteem and self-confidence into the ground. Trying to gain self-confidence and increase self-esteem while feeling guilty is like trying to fill the sieve with water.

When you have a feeling of guilt, you can twist the rope from you. And the worst thing is that there will always be people who will do this. First, a person is accused of omissions, negligence, and mistakes, with half invented and the rest exaggerated. And then they supposedly do a favor and forgive, but in fact they reckon on free work, on obligations, etc.

Feeling of guilt is released, like resentment, only more difficult. Feeling guilty is such a big resentment against yourself. I recommend first letting go of a few dozen resentments in order to gain experience before taking on the release of guilty feelings. The moment when the feeling of guilt is released - you will not confuse anything.

This is a moment of great relief, release, as if a heavy load was removed from the soul. The biggest difficulty in letting go of guilty feelings is that people really believe that they deserve it, that they themselves are guilty and should be punished.

You will be surprised, but you have no reason to feel guilty, even if you made some mistake.

And if you let go of the blame, this does not mean that you will make mistakes more often; rather, on the contrary, guilt attracts errors and problems like a magnet.

Feel free to get rid of guilt - remember no one owes anything to anyone. As you owe nothing, so are you. If you feel guilty, then you have loaded yourself with something superfluous. This is a kind of ego, look at how cool an antihero I was, could ruin the life of so many people. But deep down I'm good, so here I torment myself with guilt.

You cannot be held accountable when you feel guilty. Feeling guilty replaces responsibility. You will act extremely irresponsibly, people will be angry with you, offended, but your conscience will torment you. This is not a conscience - this is irresponsibility tormenting you. Want to be in charge? Get rid of guilt in front of others.

Exercise 10: Environment or how to be confident

Your surroundings pull you towards you. If they are Higher than you, they will pull you up. If it is lower than you, then they will accordingly be pulled down, and your confidence and self-esteem will fall. You can also choose a circle of like-minded people - those people who strive for more and really work on themselves - with such people you will also grow.

There is a category of people who need to run away - it is impossible to help them. You will not have the strength, health, or life to help them get out of the hole into which they stubbornly immerse themselves. This is not bad. This does not characterize you as bad. Save yourself and thousands will be saved around. You will try to save someone around - you will not save anyone, including yourself.

Exercise 11: A mess in the head leads to an understatement

There is such a law of nature - that which is outside is inside. (maybe one day I will describe all the laws of nature in interpersonal relations in a separate article.) If a person has a mess around, then there's also a mess in his head. I'm sorry. Living in a mess is difficult. And by the way, restoring and maintaining order around you - leads to order in the head.

I know people who have a complete mess everywhere: at the desk, garbage in the car, hostility to cleaning the house. And, "oddly enough", in personal relationships, in business relationships, in friendly relations, with children and even with parents - also a complete mess. Without enlightenment. I feel sorry for the children - they can follow in the footsteps of the parent.

Well, I understand that unwritten rules need to be violated if you want to achieve something. Serious projects cannot be implemented in a perfectly ordered office. Work on the result involves some mess. And I'm not going to dispute this. But only a working mess, as a result of a working or creative process. And not a household mess, as a result of a mess in my head.

I urge you to fight it with a household mess.

Worked - remove the excess, clean up as much as possible. Similarly at home - clean up the rooms, in the cabinets where your things are stored, in personal documents, in your car, in tools for men or in cosmetics for women, in the kitchen among dishes and accessories.

Do not strain, if you need help - find and watch several video lessons, there are a lot of them now. Buy accessories for this: different hangers, drawers, folders, shelves are now full for all occasions - all you need to bring at least some order.

Start striving for order. It can be difficult at first, then it will be natural. Learn to put the used thing in place immediately after use. This will take 3 seconds maximum. Take off your clothes - put them in their place immediately or in the laundry basket. You do not need to accumulate it on chairs, so that you can collect everything later.

Put things in order in your apartment, in cabinets, on your desktop, in things. Throw out the junk.

Use a tool or accessories - put immediately in place. Used the dishes - put immediately in the dishwasher - do not first put in the sink because it is faster for a second, then to put everything separately in the dishwasher. Adhering to this rule, you will have order, clean and will be in time much more. A lot more.

And I guarantee you you will respect yourself more, you will gain yourself, you will become more confident, your self-esteem will increase - after you put things in order around you and when you strive for order. You will gain inner strength. Self-esteem is the foundation of self-esteem and confidence.

Exercise 12: Don't Compare Yourself to Others

Probably one of the most pernicious habits for self-esteem and self-confidence is to compare yourself with others. This habit nourishes and concrets your self-doubt and low self-esteem. One way or another, everyone has this habit. Someone has more, someone less.

If you carefully observe this habit, you will notice the features. Usually, comparisons are made selectively, with those who are more advanced, with more successful, who are at a higher level, without noticing the shortcomings of the object of comparison. At home, on the contrary, flaws are looked out under a microscope when comparing.

If the object of comparison is not cool enough, then the consciousness quickly finds another, more advanced object for comparison. It turns out a priori without a winning option, lowering self-esteem and self-confidence lower and lower than the plinth. This unconscious self-torture, framed in a "sweet" BDSM habit.

Naturally, such a comparison discourages, demotivates, prevents one from acting, improving one's life, and can drive one into despair, into depression. To realize and get rid of such a habit, take a diary and watch for some time how you compare yourself with someone.

• How to choose an object for comparison?

• How do you choose what to compare between you?

• What details are you paying attention to?

• What are your advantages do not notice?

• What other flaws do you not notice?

You need to notice, recognize in the habit - all that is described above. After you have painted the details - try to do exactly the opposite: look for advantages in yourself, and the object of comparison has flaws. You will be surprised at how much of both.

Tell yourself honestly - the better you are, who are you comparing yourself to?

I am almost sure that you will find in yourself the virtues, qualities that you have underestimated in yourself so far.

Keep looking for your virtues and write in your diary. Do this every time you catch yourself comparing with someone.

Having done this exercise several times, first in writing, then it will be enough orally - you will begin to notice more advantages in yourself, while others will have more disadvantages and, in principle, will get tired of comparing yourself with someone, this is an empty matter. You will simply know that everything is fine with you. You will succeed.

form an internal ban on the use of their strengths, qualities and advantages. Over time, you stop noticing them at all. You need to bring this quality back - to notice what you are superior to others. With practice, your thinking will change, and your skill will form.

You must learn to notice the weaknesses of your competitors.

Your mind and thinking should be sharpened to identify them. And develop this skill to the smallest detail. And somewhere in the background, in your subconscious mind, your observation must constantly work to identify your advantages over others.

I am sure that you have incredibly many advantages, you just don't notice them and forbid yourself to use them. And it became a deep subconscious habit. Start changing your mindset. Find your strengths and other people's weaknesses. Allow yourself to use this for business, in order to win this competition.

Compare yourself today with yourself yesterday. This is for reference, so that you can see that you are growing, that you are moving forward. Do something every day to be better than yesterday. And with these small steps, you will gradually but ironly increase your self-esteem and self-confidence. You will be surprised how fast you will move forward and up.

Exercise 13: Stop being humble and shy

Many people overestimate modesty too much. Already too modestly consider modesty, as a benefactor, almost in the last resort. But in the current world it is impossible to succeed, possessing excessive modesty.

I want to warn you right away - I do not urge to abandon modesty at all. There is some benefit from it. But busting with modesty is extremely harmful in modern society. I urge you to abandon only "excessive modesty." And I really hope that you are smart enough to distinguish between "modesty" and "excessive modesty", because there are huge differences between them.

Excessive modesty, i.e. when there is a lot of modesty - this is nothing more than - suppression of oneself, an internal barrier, self-deception, when a flaw hiding under modesty in the form of low self-esteem and self-doubt - is presented as a virtue.

The complete lack of modesty is bad, too much modesty is also bad.

There must be some middle ground, neither more nor less. And so part of modesty you need to let go. Well, you are your own judge and you are free to choose how much modesty to leave and how much to let go - it depends on the life you want to live.

Remember situations in which you were too modest and missed something. Write them in a notebook, then disassemble in detail each individually. Find the line when modesty was too much and it began to harm. Think of how you should behave differently, so that perhaps it would not be missed?

Write in a notebook, a new model of behavior. Set yourself the mood that next time you will behave in a new way - as you yourself have chosen. All of the above applies to shyness. Busting with shyness, modesty - disguised self-suppression, erected in benefactors, which are mistakenly proud of. They should be not a lot and not a little. Do the exercise with all situations when you were too modest and shy - find an acceptable middle ground.

Exercise 14: Benefit from Criticism

Everyone needs feedback and it looks like nothing but criticism. On the other hand, criticism can be unpleasant, annoying, painful, demotivating, self-esteeming, and lowering confidence. Criticism can be useful and useless, and can be indicative.

The worst and most offensive criticism is its complete absence, which suggests that you are swimming too shallow and you are not interested in anyone. It would be better if it would be unconstructive, negative, useless - all the same, at least some benefit can be derived from this.

It follows that any criticism you receive is of HUGE value. With the growth of your self-esteem and self-confidence, you will be able to more easily tolerate harsher criticism, extracting more benefit from it.

The most dangerous criticism is only positive feedback or praise. If you are not criticized negatively, then you are too authoritarian, suppress people or they are afraid of you, therefore they prefer to keep quiet, from sin on. Only positive feedback means that you are being deceived, possibly robbed and you are missing out on something.

There are several types of criticism:

Constructive criticism or feedback.

Very valuable criticism when useful - well contributing to error correction. Available to fairly advanced people who respect you. It requires incredible efforts, life experience and wisdom to say exactly on purpose and without transitions to personalities and emotions. Often, it may take time to ponder the topic and accurately give advice.

If you find a person who can give you constructive and useful criticism, feedback - hold on to him, hands, feet, teeth, money, gifts. This is the criticism for which it is worth and must be paid, because it pays off with interest.

Often, the majority forgets to pay for such criticism and this is very, very stupid - such people also need to eat something, and even they are not fed for free. If you want more criticism, which is essentially support - pay!

If the criticism is constructive and useless, biased - means that a professional discredits you. Perhaps you are being challenged. Which is indicative of the fact that big interests or money are at stake. You grew up, you were noticed, maybe you are biting off someone else's piece or someone wants to bite you off.

Unconstructive criticism.

Over which you need to think, meditate to figure out what the critic wants to convey. It may be useful when the critic cannot express his thoughts precisely and does not fully realize what he wants to say.

It is often useless: someone wanted to be clever or pursues some other interests - it is difficult to remain silent when no one asks. Learn to completely ignore useless criticism.

Biased criticism, accusations, insults.

Very revealing situations. When you are subjected to such criticism, you are trivially deceived, discredited or want to use. You are either not there or you have seriously crossed the road for someone, they noticed you and are trying to eliminate it by dishonest methods. Well, or you stepped on the tail very and painfully for someone.

Oddly enough, but it can be useful. Perhaps you accidentally hooked someone for a living and broke through a person. Something useful from this is quite difficult to identify. Rather, such criticism is indicative - in what exactly indicative - you need to figure it out yourself. If there is no use, ignore it boldly at 100%, as if it does not exist.

The presence of such criticism from enemies and serious competitors means a big fat plus for you. Conversely, the presence of praise from competitors means a big fat minus - you miss something, make a mistake or do something wrong.

Trolls.

Mostly online. They envy you. Someone expresses his displeasure at you. Perhaps you have gathered the wrong audience, they have nothing to do, they have a lot of time, not enough money and too lazy to think - people have fun, are dumb, they are harmful.

This is indicative of criticism. Starting from some level of popularity, trolls are required, otherwise your popularity is a myth. Completely ignore what they say, write. But watch out for quantity - this is indicative. If there are no trolls, then you are still of little interest to anyone. Change your strategy - start making more confident actions.

Too much negative and emotional criticism, which a person does not have time to realize and release, can make a person a neurotic by leaps and bounds, driving into apathy, depression. However, we are not taught at school how to benefit from different types of criticism. It's a pity.

In essence, it means that education and upbringing does not teach you how to live. Only parents can teach this if they have such skills or in training. And first of all, it is your task to independently form the skills you need for a successful life. Remember - no one owes you anything, even parents.

Good feedback and soft constructive criticism - on the contrary, are leaping forward. Do not spare money for such criticism - pay, you will avoid many mistakes that will cost you tens of times more.

There are people who are completely closed from criticism and therefore for years are banging their heads in the same situations in which they periodically fall. If a person is closed, then he is closed. To criticize this is to make an enemy for yourself. If you take criticism painfully, it seems to you that everyone is bothering you - maybe you are also closed to criticism. Perform the exercise and start gradually opening.

It is vitally important for you to be able to be open and derive useful from criticism, and include detachment. Psychological armor "like in a tank", from incorrect criticism - let them beat their heads. Learn to distinguish one criticism from another. To do this, periodically analyze the situations and context of criticism that you find yourself in.

Remember now one situation when you were criticized. It is very significant why in fact it hooked you? Do not think about what the person said - think why in fact it hooked you, offended you? Very often, with painful criticism, I caught myself thinking that I myself also consider horror as I condemn myself for this.

I'm not changing anything, I pretend that everything is in order - therefore, the criticism was so catchy. Think about what mistakes you actually made? What should you do differently to avoid such situations in the future?

To some extent, every person who criticizes you is your teacher.

Exercise 15: Responsibility Equals confidence and good self-esteem.

We live in a very, very difficult time. We were not prepared for this. Now, several crises coincided in time at the same time: structural economic crisis, cultural, civilizational, demographic, religious, informational and others. We are not something that was not prepared for this - all these difficulties have created for us, one way or another, on purpose or not on purpose - it does not matter.

But you are still stronger than external shocks and problems. VERY much strength has been given to you from within to cope with all difficulties. Opportunities to succeed are still incredibly many, even in this crisis time. Raising your confidence and increasing self-esteem - you will see this.

And it does not take much time. And for everything to become available to you - you need to take responsibility for your life, for the position you are in.

You need to firmly tell yourself that you are the only one responsible for the troubles and victories that happened to you. Neither victory nor achievement was an accident. Your current situation is the result of decisions you made earlier, or inaction, as a result of your choices made earlier. Only in some cases did this lead to victories, and in others to mistakes.

If you are not mistaken, then you are not winning.

By accepting your involvement in your mistakes, you thereby unlock your inner strength. If you made a mistake, then it was you who made the victory, and not someone or something. And this is not an accident. And, therefore, if you were able to win, then now and in the future you can win!

Just keep in mind - DO NOT spread rot, condemn yourself for mistakes. It is necessary to accept oneself, although it can be difficult - otherwise it is not acceptance, but rejection of oneself. Acceptance is when you accepted a mistake, don't blame yourself for it, you're not ashamed to tell yourself - yes, I've made a mistake, I'm primarily a person.

By accepting responsibility for what is happening to you, you can change. As Karen Horney, a world-famous psychologist, said: External problems are nothing if you are strong from within.

Accept responsibility for what is happening - start doing these exercises, and your life is guaranteed to begin to improve by leaps and bounds.

Have you completed all these exercises?

Personally, I have performed this exercise dozens of times. And I know a lot of such people. By the way, not only these - I did many times more exercises. I have painted only the most necessary and effective ones for you. Life from them has changed dramatically.

And the period of life, of my youth, which should be the most beautiful part of life, is now remembered as a nightmare - because of all these silly and petty mistakes. Like a battle with your head against the wall. Like a bunch of mistakes, a lot of noise, disappointments and few results.

With each exercise performed, life got better and better. I continue to make them - life continues to improve. And oh, how nice! And I'm sure that you can significantly improve your life with these exercises! And is there anything more important than that?

Performing such an exercise means to truly value yourself and your life. This means self-respect, self-care. Getting rid of these petty troubles means to love yourself, to find yourself, to regain yourself - to squeeze a slave out of us drop by drop. The unwillingness to change, to monitor health is indicative: subconsciously (unconsciously) you do not value yourself and your life.

A person who does not do such exercises is simply deceiving himself. I hope you obviously have a nightmare and old age waiting for you if you leave all these petty bad habits?

How to complete these exercises quickly and accelerate your progress? Self-confidence training.

Now it's not enough to practice the right exercises. Life is changing too fast, getting complicated. People are overloaded with work, household chores and there is not much time left for practice, as well as strength. It is vital to achieve a quick result.

1. An environment that motivates change, or practice with like-minded people.

Internal changes are easier and faster to pass when you are in the appropriate environment, set up for the same changes as you. In such places, a chain reaction occurs when members of the group help and stimulate each other.

While your current habitat will demotivate, discredit what you do. On the other hand, it is very difficult to admit to someone that you are working on self-esteem - only very strong people are able to understand what you mean and evaluate.

95% of people do not study and do not want to change. I don't know how they will survive in 5-10 years and I think that they will face the most serious problems. Look for like-minded people and an environment in which you can open up, and which will pull you to change and gaining yourself.

I hope you enjoyed this book and exercises, and you received an exhaustive, understandable, constructive answer to the question: how to increase self-esteem and self-confidence?

• Do you agree that by applying at least half your self-confidence will increase significantly?

• Do you agree that practicing these exercises on a regular basis for another year will significantly increase your self-confidence? Namely, in 2 - 3 - 10 or more times?

• Do you agree that having completed at least part of the exercise, will your life improve significantly? Will you be less nervous, tired, make mistakes?

The only thing left is to start doing these exercises and get the result. The bad news is that, putting it now for later - you will come back to your reality and after 1-2 days will forget not only the exercises described above, but also the article in general.

You and your life will remain without the changes you desire. Perhaps you will not be able to achieve your goals and your dreams - because you lacked self-confidence. In order to change something - you need to act!

And the best time for action is now. In six months - a year you will strongly regret that you did not start doing the exercises today.

Follow the link and register for the training Doubling self-confidence in 5 lessons.

This training is the best way to start improving your life. Register now and see you at the training!

PS

Change i.e. Only active actions can improve your life - doing exercises. Exercise regularly - and then the result is guaranteed to come to you, you won't even notice it. Follow the link above, register for the training and start the practice today!

PS2

To be continued. Sign up for my newsletter. And you will be aware of my new articles, new trainings, free classes.

Dear reader
I really need your help!
If you liked my book and found useful information in it, please leave a review or review about my work on Amazon, for me as an independent author this is very important. Your feedback and support will be appreciated. It only takes a minute, and it will mean a lot to me! Hope only for you

You can follow this **<u>LEAVE A REVIEW PLEASE</u>** link on Amazon now.

Thanks in advance, **Henry Collins**

Dear Reader
I want to recommend your books:

1. HOW TO SURVIVE IN THE QUARANTINE AND DO NOT LOSE YOUR MIND
How to survive during quarantine? How to survive a pandemic shock and not go crazy in quarantine? What to do to not get depressed at all? Where is best located during quarantine? How to eat during quarantine? How not to go crazy with the whole family in isolation. Quarantined children, what to do with them? How to live so that "virusophobia" does not develop?
Addition
+11 recipes for antiseptics and hand sanitizers at home
+List of essential goods and foodstuffs of 2020 during quarantine

2. WHAT IS THE MEANING OF LIFE? A COMPLETE GUIDE TO IDENTIFYING AND SETTING LIFE GOALS
The book will help determine the purpose of life. This is a wonderful book of motivation for

women and men, a book of motivation, books menhappiness.
For a focused life, purpose and desire, the goal and strength
of women and men, as well as your hypothesis of happiness
Here are the most effective methods.